AF477831

It's Me, Mom

It's Me, Mom

By

Debi Hugill

To Chad, Kevin and Katie, you are the

joy of my life and my reason for being.

Table of Contents

I was the third of four children, born on March 19, 1953 11:34 a.m., at Mercy Hospital in Altoona PA.

My mom was in labor with me for a week. I was a blue baby and wasn't expected to live. I was so little the nurses carried me on a pillow.

I weighed barely 5 lbs.

When I was born, my godfather Jim brought a huge stuffed sheep pull toy that would baa when rolled. The nurses, who were all nuns were none too pleased. Pun intended. My godparents spoiled me rotten. I got anything I wanted, and almost all of my pretty dresses came from them.

The first house we lived in that I can remember had a porch across the front of the house. Mom would put me out on the porch in my high chair. One day, she had just taken me inside when a parked truck up the street from the house lost its brakes and crashed into the porch, wiping it out.

Guess I was supposed to survive after all.

The Holidays

When I was one or two, my sister Gail and her fiancé Dick took me to the yearly Christmas Parade in downtown Altoona. There's a picture of Dick carrying me and I'm crying. I can only assume that I didn't want the parade to end.

Christmas was always memorable ... mostly because Dad cursed loudly at the lights because they wouldn't cooperate while going on the tree. I learned so many new words that I wasn't allowed to repeat.

There was always a quaint village with a train under the tree. My Dad would use coffee grounds for the dirt on either side of the tracks. Smoke would rise from the engine stack, and the lit tree cast a multicolored glow on the train and village.

It was pretty magical except for the times that the train wouldn't run, derailed, or when a light bulb would go out on the tree. My Dad did not have the best temperament.

My greatest accomplishment was in 2nd or 3rd grade when I played Mary in the Christmas pageant.

Mom's job for Christmas was baking endless supplies of chocolate chip, raisin filled and sand tart cookies, fudge, and any other treat she could conger up. She would bake nonstop for several days, and she used Charles Chips tins for storing them. I felt that it was my job to be the taste tester on such occasions.

Each year after opening our presents on Christmas morning, we knew that we would have to keep them under the tree in their packaging. All of our aunts, uncles, cousins, and grandparents would come to our home to see our presents. My mom was the oldest of six, which lends to the understanding that there would always be a large number of relatives who would pass through our front door during the holidays. Each aunt or uncle had anywhere from four to twelve children.

One year, we decided as a family to have Christmas on Christmas Eve.

It was great until Christmas morning arrived. We felt empty and sad on the most anticipated day of the year. We never did that again.

Around the age of 3-4, I remember wondering why Kathy and Gail were freaking out about a hurricane coming our way. I was excited because I thought I'd be seeing flying candy canes in the air!

My Dad learned a lesson from me when I was 4. One should always listen to their child when they tell you that they have to use the bathroom. My dad was on the phone, ignoring me as I stood on the furnace register, pleading with him to take me upstairs to the bathroom. I knew that I wasn't allowed to climb the steep staircase on my own, and it soon became crystal clear to my dad that putting me on disregard would lead to extra work for him that day.

By age 5, I had a tricycle and rode it everywhere in the neighborhood

The bike was terribly rusted, but it got me to where I wanted to go. Going downhill was scary and fun. We had streets that rivaled the steep streets of San Francisco. Returning to the top was never as much fun as going downhill, but it never stopped me from repeating the process many times over.

I remember that on one particular Sunday, Dad took me to Sunday Mass, and I was fidgeting so much that he threatened to take me outside. I always knew what that meant, but I couldn't be still. My Dad was a big believer in corporal punishment, and I'll just leave it at that.

I started whimpering while still on the kneeler and could see that he was clenching his jaw. I realized that it was time for me to explain my fidgeting. I fought my way through the tears to tell him that my foot was under the kneeler leg and that he had all of his weight on it. I got some good guilt points for a period of time afterwards.

Every weekend, as far back as I can remember, we would go for a ride in whatever car we had at the time. Dad was always buying a different car for a multitude of reasons. We'd go to a lake, river, creek, pool, or forest for a picnic lunch or swimming. Sometimes, it was just a long Sunday drive in the country that would end at The

Meadows, the best place in the area for really good ice cream.

Dad loved anything to do with racing and belonged to a race club. His micro midget car was #9. For several years, that always took care of our Saturdays. He took me for a ride in that damn thing, and I screamed bloody murder the whole way around the track. I was 4 or 5.

There were no bathrooms at the track, but there was an

outhouse. That wasn't going to happen! My sister Kathy and I would walk through the surrounding fields and find an area to squat. At least it wasn't in our living room...

Snowy Days

Sledding was great because a neighbor would tow us with his truck back to the top of the streets so we could go again. We would get very deep snowfalls, and I would go up into our attic and open the window to hear the silence. At scheduled times each day, the sound of trains would echo in the distance. Altoona was a railroad town, and those sounds never grew old. I still stop to listen when I hear a train. We had family and friends who worked for the railroad.

Easter

Easter was always a big deal. A fancy new dress, a hat with gloves, white patent leather shoes, and ruffled ankle socks. Every Easter, we were given live, dyed chicks for our very own to keep... temporarily.

I have a vague memory of going to a farm and releasing probably the only two surviving chicks we ever had. I think whatever fateful outcomes happened throughout the years, Mom and Dad hid the evidence from us. On one particular Easter, when I was six and Rick was two, we were on the living room floor dressed to the nines eating huge chocolate bunnies. Mom was none too pleased with us because it was almost time for our Easter meal. It was tough to convince Mom that we weren't devouring the chocolate with the evidence on my face.

Depending on how early Easter came, a snowfall usually doused our excitement for the

Easter Parade of our new outfits to be viewed at Sunday Mass. We'd have to wear our winter coat and boots over our fancy new duds.

Birthdays

Birthdays were always special occasions. Mom always made scratch cakes and mine was always a banana cake with marshmallow icing. Grandparents and godparents always came for the big event, and sometimes it was just classmates and friends.

Moving

We moved to Eldorado, a pretty area in Altoona, when I was six to seven years old. Our back yard was lined with lilac bushes, and I can still smell them.

I love to tell the story of walking to school while in first grade, in the dead of winter, when the snow drifts were significantly taller than me and the temperature was 17 below zero. My kids laugh every time I tell this story.

There was a huge empty lot next to our house, and every summer, Rick and I, along with all of the neighbor kids would go outside after breakfast and didn't go back inside until dinner time. Kickball, dodgeball, baseball, tag, and catching lightning bugs.

I was at my happiest if I was covered in dirt from head to toe. If one couldn't find my location, it was always a given that I was on the tippy-top of a tree. Any tree, anywhere. I was so at home.

Up the street from our home, we had a beautiful park. Highland Park had swings, slides, a concession stand, and jukebox for dancing during the summer months. My brother-in-law Joe would always buy me candy and anything else that I wanted.

The house had a huge finished basement, and I would play dress up for hours in Gail's prom dresses and heels. I could walk in those heels back then, better than I could as an adult. Kathy had a record player and a stack of 45's in the basement that I decided I wanted to listen to. I dropped them. There were no survivors.

We had a German Shepherd named Princess who had twelve puppies, and we had to feed them formula from beer bottles. I remember how sad it was with each puppy that was sold or given away.

I had my picture taken next to some of the pups in a laundry basket. We couldn't fit all twelve into the basket. I pretended to talk on a new phone called the princess phone. It was posted in a Bell Telephone newsletter.

We moved again, and this time, to a really cool two story brick house. I loved that house. I was ten, and I had my own bedroom. Rick did, too, but he slept with me anyways, thanks to Kathy spoiling him. I spent most of my time in cherry, apple, and peach trees in those days. I was definitely a tomboy.

There was a very dramatic and incredibly sad moment in time during this period. On November 22nd, 1963 I was home from school due to an illness, and Dad was to take me to the doctor that day. We had the TV on prior to leaving for our appointment when local broadcasting was interrupted by the horrific news that our President had been shot and killed. John Fitzgerald Kennedy had been murdered in Dallas Texas. I remember thinking that Dallas must be an evil place and that I would hate it forever. I know it wasn't logical but as a ten-year-old child, that's the way I felt.

The following day, we kept the TV on all day to see what the latest news was regarding the assassination. As we watched live TV, a man named Jack Ruby shot and killed Lee Harvey Oswald who was the suspected murderer of our President. That is a moment seared into my memory forever.

    This was where I met my forever friend Barb, who lived up the road from us. We actually were in kindergarten together, and since we moved at the end of school, we lost touch but reconnected again in 5th grade.

Kindergarten. Barb and me, bottom right side. Barb is right behind me.

We spent endless hours walking the neighborhood while talking about the boys in our class or hanging out at each other's homes. One time, we walked to downtown fairly late in the evening and went up on the rooftop of Gables Department Store. To our surprise, there was a concert that night. It was the Turtles, Spencer Davis Group, and a new act called Sonny &Cher.

During the time period, Kathy and Joe got married, and along came Beth. Kathy worked nights at the concession stand of the local drive in theater and baby Beth and I would go with her. I watched whatever movie was playing while Beth slept in the back seat. Kathy would bring me all kinds of goodies from the concession stand. Best job I ever had!

We lived at that house for about two years when it was decided that we needed to move into Gram and Popop's home in nearby Juniata.

It was devastating to move away from Barb, but we found ways to still see each other. We'd walk to each other's house or we'd get a ride from one of our parents.

Soon afterwards, we were introduced to a group of fresh-faced boys, and I believe it was the beginning of what we now call pop rock. Mike Nesmith, Peter Tork, Davey Jones, and Mickey Dolenz were on TV in a silly sitcom, and we were in love! Peter was Barb's guy, and mine was Mike, also known as Wool Hat. I wore out their albums on my record player by playing them morning, noon, and night to the point that the needle on the record player wore grooves in the LP's and created skips in the songs. I taped a quarter to the needle arm to keep it from skipping, and that worked for a while.

Eventually I had to buy new copies so I could continue endless hours of listening to them. I taped a quarter to the needle arm to keep the songs from skipping, and that worked for a while. Eventually, I had to buy new copies so I could continue endless hours of listening to them.

My Gram was the best! I spent a lot of time staying with her and Popop, especially during the summer months. Gram and I would ride the bus in to town and shop at Gables Department Store. We'd end our shopping in the basement of the department store at the fountain. We'd order lime shakes and sip and talk for awhile. We'd then go to McCrory's to get hoagies to take home for our dinner with Popop. We'd board the bus for home and talk about our fun shopping spree.

Grammy would play chase with me, and we'd make Popop mad because he couldn't hear his tv programs. Gram would give me cloth samples from the silk mill that was on the next block from her home. I can still remember the great smell of the fabrics in the mill. I'd spend hours making clothes for my dolls with the material that she'd given me.

Popop had a garden, rich with Pennsylvania black soil. It literally took up most of the huge yard behind the house. He had tulip and pansy beds that were most impressive. He grew just about every vegetable there was. People would come from all over to buy his vegetables and enjoy his flower beds. I would spend time a lot of time with him in the garden. His job was tending to the garden, and mine was pulling fresh carrots or rhubarb straight out of the ground for a snack. He was my inspiration for the love of getting my hands dirty in the soil. I could tell he was proud that I was interested in gardening and that he was likely responsible.

His trade was that of a mortician, and he worked at the local funeral parlor. He also created a salve for cuts, burns and wounds. People from all over the county would drive to his home to buy his salve. He came from a long line of Pennsylvania Dutch heritage.

There was a community pool a few blocks from their house, and when I was about five years old, Gram would let me go in alone, but she'd stand on the outside on the creek bank, holding on to the chain link fence so that she could watch over me. She would stand watch for hours while I taught myself how to swim.

I adored my Grammy, and when my granddaughter Kaylee was born, I wanted her to call me Grammy. The first time she said it, it came out Gammi and it stuck.

She's the only grandchild that calls me Gammi. I'm Grandma to the other five grands. It will be interesting to see what my great-grandson calls me.

In 1968, we moved to FL. It had been a choice between Vermont and FL, and thankfully FL won out. How different my life would have been had we moved to Vermont. The apartment on Sunshine Lane had only one bedroom so Mom and Dad slept in the living/kitchen area on a sofa bed. Rick and I had twin beds in the bedroom.

School had already been in session for several weeks, so, it was scary starting a new school in a new town and a new state. In each classroom at Madeira Jr High there were windows providing a full view of Boca Ciega Bay, and I spent my class time watching dolphins playing. I didn't learn much that year. My first day of school, I was mocked for wearing pantyhose. No one in FL ever wore them! The first chance I had,

I ran into the girls' bathroom and threw them out.

It was also the year of a teacher's strike, and we had substitute teachers for most of the year. My French teacher was from Alabama. When I moved on to high school, my French teacher wanted to know what the hell language I was speaking. Apparently, I had quite the Bama drawl in my French dialect.

My future brother- in -law and I had lunch together every day in the school cafeteria, and we fended off bullies who kept making us move to a different table. I'd love to speak with them about their behavior today, but I'd likely need a visitor pass and permission from the guards to do so.

During this time period, I decided to rebel against my parents, and I changed the spelling of my name. My mother just about had a fit, but I think my dad called an audible and let it happen. So, Debbie became Debi.

My weekend days while living on Treasure Island, were spent with my friend Mary. We were always barefoot. If we weren't on the beach, we were hitching rides from college guys who were driving up and down Gulf Blvd in their rented cars. They would pick us up at the old John's Pass Bridge, and then drop us off at the Treasure Island Fun Center. From there, we'd hitch another ride back to Johns Pass. We did this all day long, and our parents never knew about it.

We moved to a house about five miles away from the beaches. Grammy and Popop moved from PA to FL, and they lived in the garage apartment behind our house. A far cry from our previous view of the Gulf of Mexico.

Once again, I shared a bedroom with Rick. This time, I was in high school. Leads to understanding why I'm so happy to have my own home and my own bedroom.

My dad drove me to high school in the mornings, and I walked home every day through my junior year until my dad got his license and a car. I carried all of my books because kids used to take anything in the school lockers.

At the age of twenty three, I became Chad's mom. He was eighteen days old when he became mine! When he was about three weeks old, I started having stomach cramps. I was pregnant and didn't know it. I had a miscarriage, and then nine months later, I was pregnant with my son

Kevin! I became a stay-at-home mom for the next three or so years.

Once the boys started school, I became a dental assistant. During my time as a dental assistant, I became pregnant, and voila, Katie! I stayed home with her for two years and then went back to work for the dentist. I stayed for another year and then went to school to become a medical assistant, working as such for one year. Entotal, I worked as a dental, then a medical assistant before becoming a nurse.

My middle name should have been assistant in those years.

At the ripe old age of thirty-eight, I started nursing school and became an LPN. I worked at Palms of Pasadena for six long months. That's when I landed a job at Hospice of the Fla Suncoast. I found my niche and never looked back. My boss was the best ever, and her son was a childhood friend of my son-in-law, small world. I started out covering for vacationing RN's. Within a short span of time, I became paired with an RN to co-case manage a caseload of patients.

I was invited to join a women's sorority for women who didn't go to college. We did charity work and raised money for All Children's Hospital. We also partied once a month and had a blast.

I've been married three, count 'em, three times. As Forrest Gump would say, that's all I have to say about that.

At the age of sixty, I spent three months studying and sat for the LPN boards for the second time, with twenty years between exams. I passed and got a new license. I didn't work at nursing again though. Shortly after passing the exam, I moved to San Jose and became a therapeutic tech to work with autistic children. Early on, I was put in a difficult situation and was asked by the company I worked for to lie to parents. THAT was my last day.

I'm proud to say that all three of my kids served our country. The long awaited year of returning home to FL was great because after decades of being apart, the kids, a few of the grandkids, and I are finally back together and home!

I am seventy years old and living my best life in my first self-owned home after some very troubled times. I have fantastic close friends from high school, and we get together for never less than three-hour lunches once a month.

My definition of a great time is any time spent with my three kids, my wonderful son in law Aaron, daughter in law Angela, mother in law Jane and six grands, three sibs, friends galore and of course, my six year old Aussiedoodle Bogie. Life is good.

Acknowledgement

To Gail, Kathy and Rick for willing and unwilling participation in my childhood.

About the Author

Debi grew up in a small railroad town in Pennsylvania and these are her childhood memories. Debi realized at the age of seventy that most children don't know their parents as anyone other than their mom or dad. Debi decided to write her memories of growing up and how she became the person she is today.